STECK-VAUGHN
PORTRAIT OF AMERICA

Arkansas

Steck-Vaughn Company
Executive Editor	Diane Sharpe
Senior Editor	Martin S. Saiewitz
Design Manager	Pamela Heaney
Photo Editor	Margie Foster
Electronic Cover Graphics	Alan Klemp

Proof Positive/Farrowlyne Associates, Inc.
Program Editorial, Revision Development, Design, and Production

Consultant: Joe David Rice, Director, Arkansas Department of Parks and Tourism

Published by Raintree Steck-Vaughn Publishers, an imprint of Steck-Vaughn Company.

A Turner Educational Services, Inc. book. Based on the Portrait of America television series by R. E. (Ted) Turner.

Cover Photo: Cover photography of Confederate Headquarters at Pea Ridge by © Raymond Barnes/Tony Stone Images.

Library of Congress Cataloging-in-Publication Data

Thompson, Kathleen.
    Arkansas / Kathleen Thompson.
       p.   cm. — (Portrait of America)
    "Based on the Portrait of America television series"—T.p. verso.
    "A Turner book."
    Includes index.
    ISBN 0-8114-7324-4 (library binding).—ISBN 0-8114-7429-1 (softcover)
    1. Arkansas —Juvenile literature. I. Title. II. Series:
Thompson, Kathleen. Portrait of America.
F411.3.T48 1996
976.7—dc20
                               95-25723
                                   CIP
                                   AC

Printed and Bound in the United States of America

3 4 5 6 7 8 9 10 WZ 02 01 00 99

Acknowledgments
The publishers wish to thank the following for permission to reproduce photographs:
P. 7 © A. C. Haralson/Arkansas Department of Parks & Tourism; p. 8 © Superstock; p. 10 Marquette University Archives; p. 11 Quapaw Quarter Association; pp. 12, 13, 14, 15 (both), 16 (both), 17 Arkansas History Commission; p. 18 U.S. Army Corps of Engineers; p. 19 (top) White House Photo, (bottom) © Tim Schick/Arkansas Department of Parks & Tourism; pp. 20, 21 UPI/Bettmann; p. 22 Arkansas History Commission; p. 23 (both) Little Rock Central High School, Little Rock School District; p. 24 © Robert Knight/Tony Stone Images; p. 26 Tyson Foods; p. 27 (both) University of Arkansas Cooperative Extension Services; p. 28 (both) Arkansas Democratic Gazette; p. 29 © A. C. Haralson/Arkansas Department of Parks & Tourism; pp. 30, 31 (both) J. B. Hunt Transport; p. 32 © A. C. Haralson/Arkansas Department of Parks & Tourism; p. 34 (top) Special Collections, University of Arkansas Libraries, University of Arkansas, Fayetteville, (bottom) © A. C. Haralson/Arkansas Department of Parks & Tourism; p. 35 (both) © A. C. Haralson/Arkansas Department of Parks & Tourism; pp. 36, 37 Blues Archive, I. D. Williams Library, University of Mississippi; pp. 38 (both), 39 © L. R. Chin/Delta Images Photography; p. 40 © Cynthia Ellis; p. 41 (left) © A. C. Haralson/Arkansas Department of Parks & Tourism, (right) Arkansas History Commission; p. 42 © Michael Reagan; p. 44 © A. C. Haralson/Arkansas Department of Parks & Tourism; p. 46 One Mile Up; p. 47 (left) One Mile Up, (center, right) Arkansas Department of Parks & Tourism.

STECK-VAUGHN
PORTRAIT OF AMERICA

Arkansas

Kathleen Thompson

A Turner Book

RSVP
RAINTREE
STECK-VAUGHN
PUBLISHERS
The Steck-Vaughn Company

Austin, Texas

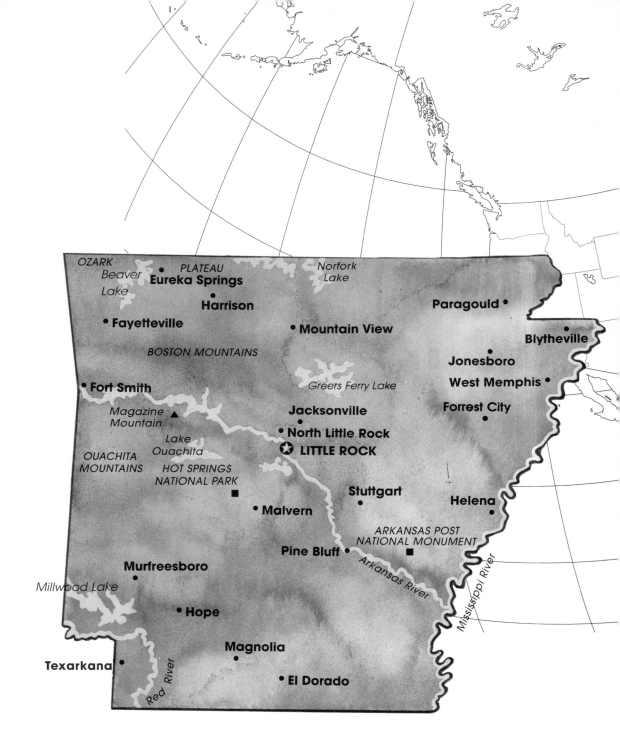

Arkansas

OZARK PLATEAU
Beaver Lake
Eureka Springs
Harrison
Fayetteville
BOSTON MOUNTAINS
Norfork Lake
Paragould
Mountain View
Blytheville
Jonesboro
Greers Ferry Lake
West Memphis
Fort Smith
Forrest City
Magazine Mountain ▲
Jacksonville
Lake Ouachita
North Little Rock
⭐ **LITTLE ROCK**
OUACHITA MOUNTAINS
HOT SPRINGS NATIONAL PARK ■
Stuttgart
Helena
Malvern
ARKANSAS POST NATIONAL MONUMENT ■
Murfreesboro
Pine Bluff
Arkansas River
Mississippi River
Millwood Lake
Hope
Magnolia
Texarkana
Red River
El Dorado

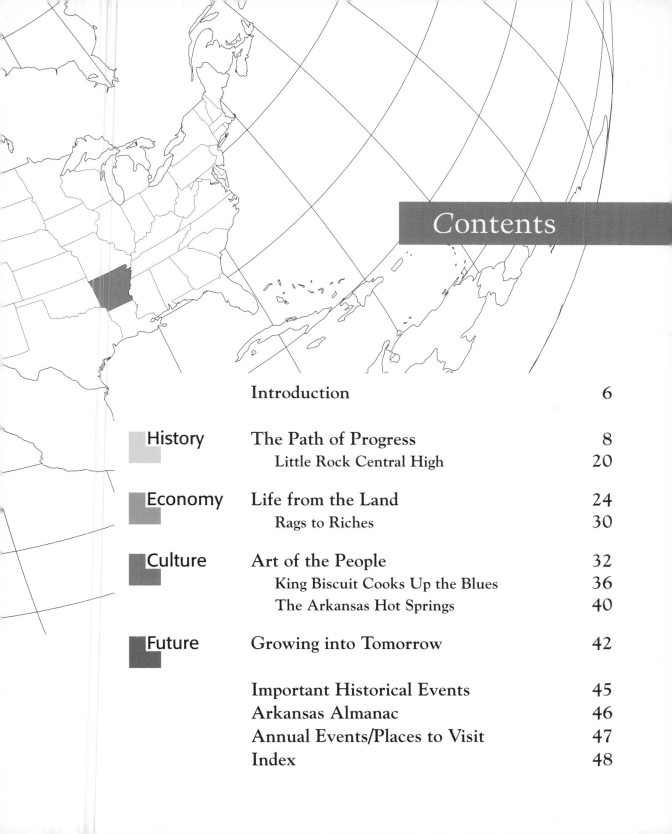

Contents

Introduction   6

History   The Path of Progress   8
    Little Rock Central High   20

Economy   Life from the Land   24
    Rags to Riches   30

Culture   Art of the People   32
    King Biscuit Cooks Up the Blues   36
    The Arkansas Hot Springs   40

Future   Growing into Tomorrow   42

Important Historical Events   45
Arkansas Almanac   46
Annual Events/Places to Visit   47
Index   48

Introduction

Arkansas is nicknamed "the Natural State." The nickname is not surprising because many of the state's economic opportunities come from its natural resources. Arkansas is a nature-lover's paradise. Fishers, swimmers, and boaters love to splash in its rivers, lakes, and springs. These same water resources also provide the state with hydroelectric power. Hikers and campers enjoy the beautiful mountains. These same mountains are home to acres of forests, which provide the state with lumber and paper products. Important minerals, natural gas, and petroleum are found in the southern portion of the state. Arkansas makes the most of the opportunity from the best of nature's bounty.

These hikers are climbing to the top of Buffalo Rock in the Ozark Mountains of Arkansas.

The Path of Progress

About 10,000 years ago, early hunters lived in the area we now call Arkansas. These were nomadic people, which means that they didn't settle in one place for long. Instead they followed the migrations of animals that they killed for food and clothing. Around 8000 B.C. these people began to make permanent homes in the foothills of the Ozark mountains, in the western part of present-day Arkansas. They built their shelters beneath overhanging rocks called bluffs, so they came to be called the Bluff Dwellers.

About 1000 B.C. people called the Mound Builders began to settle in the eastern part of the state. These people built huge earthen mounds that supported homes and religious structures. Other mounds were used for burial sites. The Mound Builders had mysteriously disappeared from the area by the sixteenth century.

The Spanish explorer Hernando de Soto arrived in Arkansas in 1541. The area was then inhabited by

The Old State House in Little Rock was the state capitol building from 1836 until 1911. It is now a museum of Arkansas history.

many different Native American groups. De Soto had been sent by Spain to find gold in the southeastern part of North America. He spent about a year exploring the Arkansas area. When he found no gold, he traveled south to try his luck in present-day Louisiana.

Well over 125 years later, in 1673, French explorers Father Jacques Marquette and Louis Jolliet and their Native American escorts canoed down the Mississippi River from Canada. They reached the Arkansas River before turning back. France sent René-Robert Cavelier, Sieur de La Salle, along the same path in 1682. La Salle sailed down the Mississippi River to the Gulf of Mexico, then claimed the entire Mississippi Valley for France. This area included all the land fed by the Mississippi River and its tributaries. Much of this land La Salle had never seen, and all of it was already occupied by Native Americans. He named this huge area Louisiana, in honor of King Louis XIV. Louisiana included all of present-day Arkansas.

In 1686 Henri de Tonti, one of the officers in La Salle's party, built Arkansas' first permanent European settlement, called Arkansas Post. France attempted to establish a few other settlements, but none lasted more than a few years. France granted Louisiana to Spain in 1762. From 1775 to 1783, the Revolutionary War raged to the east, and the American colonists won their independence from Great Britain. Spain joined the colonists in their war and defended Arkansas against the British in 1783 with help from the Quapaw, a Native American group. In 1800 Spain transferred Louisiana back to France.

Father Jacques Marquette, shown here, traveled with Louis Jolliet down the Mississippi River from Canada. The two explorers and their crew made the entire journey by canoe.

In 1803 France sold Louisiana to the United States at an extremely low price—about $15 million. Once Louisiana belonged to the United States, many more settlers moved into the Arkansas area.

The primary crop grown by settlers in Arkansas and throughout the South was cotton. The climate in the South was just right for growing cotton. Cotton was profitable because of the demand for it in Great Britain and in the New England states, which needed cotton for textile manufacturing. Also, the cotton gin, patented by Eli Whitney in 1794, increased the output of cotton. This machine could separate cotton fibers from seeds as rapidly as fifty workers could. Plantation owners used slaves to work the land.

This restored Victorian building is in the Quapaw Quarter of downtown Little Rock. Many buildings in the Quapaw Quarter date from before the Civil War.

By 1819 Arkansas had nearly 15,000 settlers, and the United States Congress approved it as an official territory. Cotton and the slave system used to produce it were at the root of a major controversy by this time, however. Northern and southern states were arguing over whether slavery should be allowed in new territories and states. The North wanted Arkansas to be a free territory, but the South wanted to expand their cotton production—and that meant expanding slave labor. In 1820 the Missouri Compromise solved the disagreement by declaring all new territories above the northern border of Arkansas—except Missouri—free states. That meant that slavery was allowed in Arkansas. The Arkansas Territory included all of today's Arkansas and part of Oklahoma.

During these territorial years, Congress decided that American settlers needed more land. Beginning around 1830 all Native Americans in Arkansas and throughout the Southeast were forced to move west into an area of present-day Oklahoma called the "Indian Territory." Many Native Americans died of exhaustion, starvation, and disease during the journey.

American settlers had taken over the land that the Native Americans were forced to leave, and the population reached about fifty thousand. In 1836 Arkansas officially became a state. James S. Conway became the first governor of the state, and Little Rock was the capital.

By 1840 almost all Native Americans had been forced out of Arkansas. The population of settlers had nearly doubled in the four years since statehood, reaching about one hundred thousand. By 1850 Arkansas, northwest Louisiana, and east Texas were the most prosperous and rapidly growing plantation regions. By 1860 Arkansas' population reached about 430,000. About a quarter of these people were slaves.

Abraham Lincoln became President of the United States in 1861. The southern states disagreed with his views on slavery and states' rights, the amount of control the federal government had over the states. By February 1, 1861, seven states, all of them from the South, had withdrawn from the Union. These states set up their own nation, which they called the

Arkansas organized its first railroad company in 1853. Railroads replaced steamboats in the state around 1890 as the top form of commercial transportation.

Confederate States of America. Although Arkansas was a slave state, many people in the northern part of the state didn't own slaves. They wanted to remain in the Union. In March 1861, Arkansas legislators voted to stay in the Union. When President Lincoln called for Union troops, however, Arkansas legislators decided that they couldn't fight against their Southern neighbors. This time, in a 69 to 1 vote, Arkansas withdrew from the Union. Three other states joined the Confederacy, bringing the total to 11 states. About 14,000 Arkansas men, including 5,500 African Americans, joined the Union Army anyway. About sixty thousand from the state, however, fought for the Confederacy.

In 1863 the Union Army captured Little Rock. A Union government was established a year later. The Confederates moved the state capital to the town of Washington, southwest of Little Rock. So Arkansas had two state governments until the end of the Civil War in 1865.

Union troops fought to capture Little Rock from the Confederacy in September 1863. Their victory forced the Confederates to start a new Confederate state capital southwest of the city.

The period after the Civil War was called Reconstruction. It was a difficult time for the South. Many Southerners had lost their homes and farms, and the economy was ruined. President Lincoln had a plan to help the South get back on its feet. But Lincoln was killed by a Confederate sympathizer a few days after the end of the war. The task of Reconstruction fell to a group of politicians known as the Radical Republicans, who believed that former Confederates should be punished for leaving the Union.

The Radical Republicans enacted many positive changes for the South. In Arkansas they helped pass laws to grant African American men full citizenship, including the right to vote. They also helped set up the state's first free public schools. There were some negative effects, too. For one thing, the militia that was put in place to enforce laws in Arkansas often acted above the law. In addition, the Radical Republicans mismanaged the state's funds so badly that in only a few years, the state had become bankrupt.

In June 1868, Arkansas became the second Southern state to be readmitted to the Union. But former Confederates were still angry at their

Sharecroppers farmed and lived on someone else's land. They received a small share of the crop for their work. The rest belonged to the landowner.

harsh treatment by the Radical Republicans. Many joined a group called the Ku Klux Klan. This racist group began a reign of terror against African Americans and any others who dared to support them. It was a violent time for Arkansas and for the South.

Elisha Baxter, on the left, was forced out of the Arkansas State House at gunpoint by Joseph Brooks, on the right.

Violence even made its way into the Arkansas government. In 1872 Elisha Baxter was elected governor of Arkansas. But his opponent, Joseph Brooks, believed that he had won instead. After Baxter had been in office for two years, Brooks gathered his own militia and forced Baxter out of the Arkansas State House. Brooks then set up barricades around the State House to defend his new post, while Baxter assembled two thousand people to fight for his side. Baxter regained the State House after about a month, and later a federal investigation defended his position. But about two hundred Arkansas residents lost their lives in what is known as the "Brooks-Baxter War."

Elisha Baxter was the last Republican governor of Arkansas for almost one hundred years. Once Democrats regained the government in the election of 1874, they almost immediately began to reverse the Republican policies that had been enacted during Reconstruction. Within a few years, conservative Democrats had managed to take away most of what African Americans had gained. By 1891 "Jim Crow laws" denied African Americans equal access to

Bauxite, used to make aluminum, was discovered in 1887, near Little Rock.

Hattie Caraway was the first woman to be elected to the United States Senate. She represented Arkansas from 1931 to 1945.

restaurants, trains, and even water fountains. Poll taxes, which required voters to pay a tax, discouraged African Americans and other poor people from voting.

The economy of Arkansas boomed briefly after Reconstruction. The entry of the United States into World War I in 1917 also helped, as the demand increased for crops and manufactured goods to supply soldiers overseas. Almost seventy thousand Arkansas soldiers served in the war. Two thousand of them sacrificed their lives.

In 1927 flooding of the Mississippi and Arkansas rivers devastated the state's richest farmlands and even drowned much of the area's livestock. Then the opposite problem struck in 1930, when a severe drought killed many crops that had just begun to revive. The state's economy might have survived if the Great Depression hadn't come at the same time.

The Depression was a severe nationwide economic slump. Farms and factories across the nation were forced to cut production or close. Countless people lost their jobs and were left without enough money for even such necessities as food and clothing. Banks failed, which meant that people lost money they had saved. By 1933 Arkansas' economy was nearly bankrupt.

That same year President Franklin D. Roosevelt was sworn into office. Roosevelt helped put people in Arkansas and the rest of the country back to work by setting up federal programs to build public buildings, roads, and waterways. The Roosevelt administration also helped farmers develop more effective methods to increase their production.

Arkansas and the nation were at last nearly recovered economically when World War II began in 1939. Industry slowly became more important than agriculture to the economy of Arkansas, as more and more factories were built to supply the needs of overseas troops. Arkansas' natural resources, such as oil, natural gas, and bauxite, which is used to make aluminum, were also in great demand during the war.

Problems returned to Arkansas in the 1950s. In 1954 the Supreme Court of the United States ruled that public schools could not be segregated, meaning that schools couldn't keep students from attending because of their race. In 1957 nine African American students in Arkansas decided to test the Supreme Court ruling by enrolling in Little Rock Central High School.

Governor Orval E. Faubus held many press conferences to defend his position on the Little Rock Central High School controversy. He made his fight against desegregation the main platform for his successful reelection campaign that year.

Governor Orval E. Faubus called in the Arkansas National Guard to keep the students out of the school. After three weeks President Dwight D. Eisenhower sent in federal troops to escort the students safely to class. Despite the victory of these nine students, however, Arkansas' public schools weren't fully integrated for another ten years.

A policy of desegregation was pursued under Winthrop Rockefeller, the state's first Republican governor since Reconstruction. Elected in 1966, Rockefeller also worked with the legislature to put in place the state's first minimum wage law, raise teachers' salaries, and institute prison reform.

Another important development around this time was the completion of the McClellan-Kerr Arkansas River Navigation System in 1970. This waterway up the Arkansas River from the Mississippi River to Oklahoma helps control flooding and provides hydroelectric power. The waterway has also boosted Arkansas' economy by making it possible for mines and factories to ship their goods more easily by barge.

But not everyone in Arkansas has benefited from the improved economy. The people of Arkansas are, on average, the fourth poorest in the nation. About one fifth of them, including nearly one quarter of the state's children, live below the poverty level.

Arkansas residents hope that recent educational reforms will help improve

The McClellan-Kerr Arkansas River Navigation System was the largest project the United States Army Corps of Engineers ever attempted. The Corps completed the project in 1970.

opportunities for the poor. The people of Arkansas used to be among the least educated in the nation. But Bill Clinton, who served as governor from 1979 to 1981 and from 1983 to 1992, helped to remedy that problem.

As governor, Clinton instituted a number of educational reforms, including basic skills tests for public school teachers and students. He also worked to keep students in high school by passing a law to take away the driver's licenses of dropouts. Today, more students in Arkansas finish high school than in any other state in the South.

The people of Arkansas were sorry to lose Bill Clinton to the presidency of the United States in 1992, but they are proud to show off their state as an example of his success. Their continued dedication to education, along with increased attention to poverty and racial strife, have brought Arkansas into the spotlight in recent years as one of the most promising states in the South.

Bill and Hillary Clinton made an appearance during Bill Clinton's campaign for President of the United States. At age 46 Clinton became the third youngest person ever to hold that office.

Little Rock, which was established in 1820, has become a modern metropolis. It is a marketing and manufacturing center and the state's largest city.

Little Rock Central High

In May 1954 the Supreme Court of the United States made a monumental decision. The nine justices voted unanimously to outlaw segregation in the nation's public schools. Segregation is the separation of people by race. "To separate them [African American children] solely because of their race," wrote Chief Justice Earl Warren, "generates a feeling of inferiority . . . that may affect their hearts and minds in a way unlikely ever to be undone." Most schools in the South were very upset with this decision. Except for a few schools in Texas and Arkansas, legislators across the South ignored the ruling and continued to educate African American children in separate schools, just as they had done for years.

The school board of Little Rock, Arkansas, was more progressive than most in the South. They began planning the integration of their district right away. But it took three years for the plan to be put into place. Many parents and students in the district still disagreed with the United States

Elizabeth Eckford is turned away by the Arkansas National Guard as she tries to enter Little Rock Central High School.

Supreme Court ruling. At last, in 1957, nine African American students enrolled in Little Rock Central High School. They would soon be known as the "Little Rock Nine."

On September 4 the nine students arrived at Little Rock Central High for their first day of school. They were greeted by a threatening mob of people who didn't want them there. They were also met by the Arkansas National Guard. Governor Orval E. Faubus had called in the guard—not to help the students get into school safely but to be sure they stayed out of school. The Little Rock Nine were forced to return home.

It took an order from President Dwight D. Eisenhower to get the students into school. Three weeks after the first day of school, Eisenhower ordered one thousand federal troops to Little Rock. On September 25 the students at last walked through the doors of Little Rock Central. Each was assigned a soldier as an escort. They made it through the day and went home shaken but proud. One day had been hard enough, but they still had a whole school year ahead!

Elizabeth Eckford was one of the Little Rock Nine. She vividly remembered her year as a junior at Little Rock Central. "Every day it was something," she said, "and often I cried because of the torment that my parents and I went through. . . . [But] even though there was a screaming mob outside of that school every day, there were a lot more people—families and people that I didn't know—who supported us." As difficult as it was, Eckford and her

Guarded by federal troops, African American students climb the steps of Little Rock Central High School on September 25, 1957.

eight friends were determined to finish out the year.

Ernest Green was the only one of the Little Rock Nine attending as a senior. On May 27, 1958, he became the first African American student to graduate from Little Rock Central. On the night of the graduation ceremony, the school principal suggested that he mail Green's diploma, rather than risk any violence. But Green didn't go through that year for nothing. "I'm sorry," he told the principal. "My family came to see me graduate and I won't disappoint them." He remembered

An angry crowd follows Elizabeth Eckford as she approaches Little Rock Central High School.

thinking as he walked to the podium to accept his diploma, "I am walking not only for me, but for all nine of us."

Six of the other eight students were ready to enter Little Rock Central as seniors in the fall of 1958. But Governor Faubus decided that he would rather close Little Rock's public high schools than allow African Americans to attend another year. The controversy at last came to an end in 1959 when the schools gave in to federal pressure to open their doors to all students. But it took many years for Little Rock Central to welcome its African American students as warmly as the rest.

Marie McNeil is the Social Studies Supervisor for the Little Rock School District. She first came to Little Rock from New York City as a young woman fresh out of college. She wanted to teach at Little Rock Central High. "When my family heard that I had decided to come to Arkansas, they had a fit," remembered McNeil. But she was determined to bring her talents as a teacher to that school.

It soon became part of McNeil's mission as a teacher to give her students pride in themselves and in

The student population of Little Rock Central High School, the site of one of the nation's worst desegregation clashes, is now well over half African American. In addition about a third of the school's teachers are also African American.

Little Rock Central High School has laid the past to rest with a commitment to quality education for students of all races.

their state. That pride began with freeing themselves from the past. "People still think of Arkansas as Little Rock Central, 1957. I think it has affected a lot of students at times. We constantly see people driving up in front of the school, taking pictures, and thinking, 'Well, I wonder what it was like in 1957.' Little Rock Central is not like 1957."

It certainly isn't. In fact about 60 percent of the students enrolled at Little Rock Central in 1997 were African American. With the help of teachers like Marie McNeil, people are beginning to recognize Little Rock Central High for its promising future instead of its past.

Life from the Land

Life in Arkansas is, and always has been, closely tied to the land. From the early 1790s until the Civil War, cotton was the most important moneymaker in the state. Arkansas remained an agricultural state well into the twentieth century. Today, however, agriculture is no longer the state's major economic activity. Most of the people work in factories, stores, and offices. But in Arkansas, even manufacturing depends on the land.

Manufacturing is the leading source of income for Arkansas, bringing in about $13 billion annually. Two of the three most important areas of manufacturing— food processing and paper products—are tied directly to products grown from the soil. Most of the state's food-processing employees work for one company, Tyson Foods. Tyson employs over twenty thousand Arkansas workers. They process and package products such as chickens, snack foods, and frozen dinners. In all, there are about 350 food-processing plants in Arkansas, which process a variety of agricultural products.

The Joe T. Robinson Memorial Auditorium in Little Rock was opened in 1940 and renovated in 1972 and 1982.

Tyson Foods, Inc., processes chickens and other food products in over twenty plants across Arkansas. The company has many more plants across the nation.

Making paper products is the second most important manufacturing industry in Arkansas. Over half of Arkansas is forested, supplying plenty of raw material for the more than one hundred paper-manufacturing companies in the state. Georgia-Pacific and International Paper Company are the two largest paper companies in Arkansas and employ about eight thousand workers.

Farming doesn't earn nearly as much money as manufacturing does in Arkansas. In addition the number of farms in Arkansas is gradually shrinking; there are about eighteen percent fewer farms since the 1980s. But farming is still crucial to the economy of Arkansas. There are about 46,000 farms in the state, which cover about 42 percent of its total land area. All these farms produce more than $5.3 billion worth of crops and livestock products each year.

Livestock, especially chicken for broiling, is the largest agricultural industry in Arkansas. In fact Arkansas raises over one billion chickens each year— more than any other state. Arkansas is also one of the country's leading egg producers. Beef cattle are another important livestock product, as are turkeys, hogs, and dairy cattle.

The state's most valuable crop is soybeans. About 81 million bushels of soybeans are grown in Arkansas each year. Rice is next in importance. In fact Arkansas raises more rice than any other state in the nation. Arkansas farmers grow about eight billionpounds of rice each year. Although cotton has lost its importance since the state's early farming days, it's still a crucial

This combine is harvesting rice. Arkansas produces about one third of the rice grown in the United States.

crop. Only four states in the nation grow more cotton than Arkansas. Wheat, corn, hay, and sorghum grain are other main Arkansas crops.

Arkansas' minerals, especially coal, oil, and bauxite, were almost as important as cotton in the state's early economy. Today's main minerals are natural gas, oil, and bromine. Most important is natural gas, which comes mostly from the northwestern part of the state. Second in importance is oil. Arkansas produces about eight million barrels of oil each year. Third most important is the element bromine, which is used in pesticides, gasoline, dyes, and medicine. In fact Arkansas produces more bromine than anywhere else in the world. In all about four thousand of Arkansas' workers mine the land.

Some of the most important industries in Arkansas do not create any product at all. These are called service industries. Service industries are those in which workers help people or perform tasks for them instead of producing or

In the 1960s it took Arkansas farmers 56 days to raise a three-pound broiler chicken. With today's modern methods, farmers can raise a four-pound chicken in only 41 days.

Sam Walton's original variety store, Walton's, opened in 1945.

Wal-Mart founder Sam Walton was proud of his company's success. Wal-Mart is one of the largest retailers in the United States.

processing things. About two out of every three of the state's workers are employed in some type of service industry. Some examples of service workers are grocery clerks, real estate agents, doctors, and bus drivers.

Wholesale and retail trade is the most important category of service industries in Arkansas. Wholesale trade is the sale of large quantities of goods, mostly to companies such as car dealerships, grocery stores, and department stores. Retail trade is the sale of small quantities of goods, mostly to people rather than companies. Customers who buy a car, a bag of groceries, or a new pair of jeans are participating in retail trade. Arkansas' two most important retail establishments are Wal-Mart discount stores and Dillard's department stores. Both of these stores were established in Arkansas and went on to become national enterprises. Wal-Mart was started by Arkansan Sam Walton. Wholesale and retail trade together produce about 17 percent of the state's revenue each year.

Two other categories of service industries have an equal importance to the state. One category includes finance, insurance, and real estate. Workers in this category include bankers, insurance agents, and real estate agents. The other category has to do with community, social, and personal services. Doctors and nurses, mechanics, lawyers, and hotel employees are some of the workers in this area. Arkansas service industries account for almost 70 percent of the state's Gross State Product.

Tourism, one of the most important areas of the Arkansas economy, involves many types of service workers. Some Arkansans involved in the tourism industry are motel clerks, information booth workers, souvenir store cashiers, and restaurant servers. Arkansas has worked hard to promote its tourist attractions. As a result, tourism revenue in Arkansas has nearly doubled since the 1980s. Visitors spend over three billion dollars in the state every year.

Arkansas has changed with the changing times. Today, more economic opportunities are opening up all over the state. New skills and new jobs mean a healthier future for Arkansas.

Pristine landscapes such as this one are among the attractions for tourists in Arkansas. Thousands visit the state's 50 state parks/museums each year.

Rags to Riches

J. B. Hunt grew up in a small Arkansas town during the Great Depression. He sacrificed his education to help his family survive, leaving school at age 12. "We was poor share-croppers, you know," said Hunt. "We got up way before daylight and worked 'til dark. So we worked ten to twelve hours a day, six days a week. And the only money we had for clothes or anything is what we worked picking cotton for other people."

J. B. Hunt's trucks haul large amounts of food and paper products, two of the major products of Arkansas.

As Hunt grew older, he worked at any odd jobs he could find to help his family. He worked as a sawmill opera- tor, a field hand in the Arkansas cotton fields, and a livestock auctioneer. He began driving trucks in his twenties, when he moved to Little Rock on a borrowed ten dollars. After ten years as a driver, Hunt felt he had learned enough to start his own trucking company.

J. B. Hunt Transport was founded in 1969 with only five trucks. Hunt lost $19,000 that first year, but he refused to give up. The next year he managed to make a profit, and there hasn't been a down year since.

Today, J. B. Hunt Transport is one of the ten largest trucking companies in the United States. The company now owns 8,000 trucks and more than 22,000 trailer attachments. Over 12,000 people work for the company in the United States, Canada, and Mexico. Hunt wants to give all of these workers the opportunity to be as successful as he has been.

"I want everybody to be rich," said Hunt. "You know, it's like fresh air that I never had before. Now I've got it. Now I want my fellow workers to

J. B. Hunt Transport Services, Inc., fell $19,000 into debt in its first year. Today, the company makes about $1.5 billion each year.

come on up here and breathe some of this good stuff with me."

And J. B. Hunt does more for his workers than just pay them well. They also know that the boss is going to greet them when he meets them in the hallway. They get advice from the boss about how to invest their money. They have someone paying attention to them and to their lives.

"Just paying a guy and you don't care what happens to him is terrible," said Hunt. "And I think we have the ability to get these people fired up, get them to work harder, save more, do more, get out there, you know, and do a better job. And everybody wins. And that's part of my plan. Because when I die, I

should have at least one hundred millionaires working for me." J. B. Hunt doesn't think that anyone should have to go through what he did just to become a millionaire. The rewards should come from hard work alone.

J. B. Hunt Transport is one of the fastest-growing businesses in the United States.

Art of the People

The days of the antebellum, or pre-Civil War, South are long gone. But the flavor of that time hasn't been erased from Arkansas' culture. In fact it has been incorporated into a powerful culture that brings the state's history into a new light. From quiltmaking and storytelling to fiddling and composing, the best parts of Arkansas' heritage have been preserved or restored for the present.

Little Rock is a popular place for the classical arts, hosting the state's orchestra, theater, opera, and choral ensembles. But it's the folk arts of the Ozarks in the west and the blues of the Delta in the east that make the culture of Arkansas unique. Festivals that combine folk crafts and music take place in the Ozarks region yearly. The Arkansas Folk Festival at Mountain View and the Fiddlers Jamboree in Harrison are two of the region's biggest events. Just as popular are the yearly blues festivals in the eastern part of the state. One of the largest of these is the King Biscuit Blues Festival held in Helena every October.

The skills for making Arkansas crafts and folk art have been handed down over many generations.

William Grant Still was the first major African American composer in the United States.

Many of Arkansas' artists have used the state's rich history as a base for their creativity. Born in Little Rock, poet and writer John Gould Fletcher centered much of his work in his home state. One of Fletcher's best-known books is a collection of poems called *The Epic of Arkansas*, which captures scenes and stories from Arkansas' past. His *Selected Poems* won the Pulitzer Prize in 1939.

Johnny Cash is a singer, songwriter, and musician who also has carried on Arkansas' heritage. Cash was born south of Little Rock, and his musical roots speak of the country folk of the southern Arkansas flatlands. His career has earned him a place in the Country Music Hall of Fame.

Many of Arkansas' artists have drawn from the state's history of racial strife. One such writer was Eldridge Cleaver, who was born near Little Rock in 1935. One of the leaders of the African American activist group, the Black Panthers, Cleaver wrote about his feelings of alienation in American society. His 1968 book *Soul on Ice* was his most famous work.

Another Arkansas artist who focused much of his work on the struggles of African Americans was William Grant Still. Born in Mississippi but raised in Arkansas, Still composed symphonies, ballets, and operas. His most famous piece is *Afro-American Symphony*, which in 1931

These children are about to perform in Newport's 1994 Port Fest.

became the first African American symphonic composition ever to be performed by a professional orchestra.

Writer and historian Dee Alexander Brown was born in Louisiana and grew up in Little Rock, but his most famous book was about the American West. Some of Brown's friends in his youth were Native Americans. Because of these friends, Brown came to realize that almost all portrayals of Native Americans in books and movies were from the viewpoint of settlers and soldiers. Brown wrote *Bury My Heart at Wounded Knee*, a historical book about the settlement of the West, from the Native American point of view. The book has since sold over five million copies.

Arkansas storytellers bring highlights of the state's mountain culture into the spotlight. Vance Randolph, who lived in the Ozark mountains, collected and published many mountain legends and "tall tales." His best-known collection is called *We Always Lie to Strangers*, a title that empha- sizes the mischievous humor of the Ozark people.

Arkansas roots run deep. The people of the state take great pride in showing off their cultural heritage. And why not? It shows the humor and the sadness, the rhythm and the harmonies of a life that has not faded, but rather grown, over time.

Arkansas never closes its sports-fishing season. This man is fishing on Lake Ouachita, one of the purest natural lakes in the country.

Visitors at Crater of Diamonds State Park can mine for diamonds and keep whatever gems they find. About three diamonds per day are found in this mine.

King Biscuit Cooks Up the Blues

Rice Miller—better known as Sonny Boy Williamson II—was perhaps the greatest blues harmonica player that ever lived.

Every year on the second weekend of October, an estimated fifty thousand people flock to downtown Helena, Arkansas, on the banks of the Mississippi River. The attraction is the King Biscuit Blues Festival, where a great variety of blues artists play and sing the blues—for free. How did such a popular music festival get started in such a small eastern Arkansas town?

The answer has to do both with the history of the blues and the history of Helena.

The fertile area surrounding the Mississippi River in both Arkansas and Mississippi is known as the Mississippi Delta. By 1900 a new kind of music had evolved in the area. People called it the Delta Blues, and it had grown out of many earlier styles of African American folk music. The blues at that time usually featured a singer and an instrument, such as a piano or a guitar. The blues' lyrics were often about life's hardships, male and female relationships, or the need to pack up and "move on."

In 1930 Helena was a town where money could be made. Poor rural African Americans from Mississippi came to the town to find employment at the boatyard, cotton-processing plant, railroad yards, and the other industries that made Helena an economic center. It had also become a blues center. Blues musicians from all over the Delta area played in Helena's cafes and clubs, exchanging playing styles and sharing musical ideas. Because of the exchange of ideas, the blues changed and developed.

In 1941 a man named Sam Anderson decided that the town deserved its own radio station. Two musicians, harmonica player Sonny Boy Williamson II and guitarist Robert Junior Lockwood, approached Anderson about the possibility of playing their music on the air. Anderson told them they would need someone to sponsor them, that is, cover the costs of producing the radio show. Williamson and Lockwood succeeded in getting the Interstate Grocery Company to sponsor a radio show that would feature blues music. Interstate Grocery distributed King Biscuit Flour, and the show was called "King Biscuit Time."

Williamson was a phenomenal harmonica player as well as a good showman. Lockwood had a unique and dazzling way of playing his guitar. Like many other Delta bluesmen, Lockwood sometimes used a slide on his guitar—a glass bottleneck or piece of metal that he would slide along the neck of the guitar to create a haunting effect. The talents of Williamson and Lockwood made "King Biscuit Time" on Helena's new station, KFFA, a huge success. It brought the blues to anyone who had a radio within forty or fifty miles of the station.

Helena became an even bigger center for the blues during the 1940s, because so many blues musicians were eager to have their music broadcast. Consequently many famous blues musicians got their start in Helena. James Cotton, Sunnyland Slim, Pinetop Perkins, B. B. King, and Elmore James all played on "King Biscuit Time." The

Robert Junior Lockwood started playing the guitar at age 7. He learned from his stepfather, Robert Johnson, who was also a famous blues musician.

A great number of popular blues musicians have Sonny Boy Williamson to thank for the widespread popularity of the blues.

blues thrived, and many new styles and innovations influenced and transformed the music. From blues came boogie-woogie, swing, and other jazz forms that developed during the 1950s and 1960s. In the 1960s, rock 'n' roll groups, such as the Rolling Stones and Led Zeppelin, recorded and popularized their own versions of Delta Blues songs.

Because Helena had played a role in the shaping of modern blues and had been the home of many blues legends, townspeople thought a blues festival would be an ideal way to celebrate the town's history. Helena's first King Biscuit Blues Festival took place in 1986. Fifteen thousand people came that first year, and the festival was judged to be a success. The festival has become an annual event, each year attracting more people who travel greater distances to get to the festival. Some visitors even come from outside of the United States. Over the years the festival has developed into a four-day event, offering other forms of entertainment as well as the blues. In 1994 a gospel stage featured singers from twenty different gospel groups. The festival also sponsors a blues talent contest, barbecue-cooking contests, arts and crafts, an eight-kilometer run, children's events, and exhibits of local art works.

The blues make up a large part of Helena's identity throughout the year. "King Biscuit Time" still airs every weekday on KFFA. It is the longest running blues show ever and has broadcast more than ten thousand shows. Helena's blues fans have also set up the Sonny Boy Blues Society. The society has plans for establishing a blues museum in Helena. It has also created a "Blues in the Schools" program that teaches students the elements of playing blues music. Perhaps Charlie Musselwhite, a noted Delta harmonica player, best sums up the way many people feel about the town. "The whole of Helena looks pretty much like it did all through the '40s and '50s. And it's just a great feeling to be walking through that old town . . . and hear the blues just floating over the city."

People from all over the world come to Helena for the King Biscuit Blues Festival. A recent festival drew about fifty thousand visitors.

The Arkansas Hot Springs

Until the beginning of this century, most people who wanted to take a hot bath had to first carry water from a river or a well. Then they gath- ered wood to start a fire, heated the water in a big pot, and poured it into a tub. For thousands of years, taking a hot bath was rare and enjoyed mostly by the rich. Considering all that hard work, it's easy to see why a place where hot water bubbles out of the ground naturally would seem wonderful! In such a place all a bather has to do is step into the water. What a luxury!

Such an amazing place exists at Hot Springs National Park in Arkansas' Ouachita Mountains. There, over one million gallons of hot water flow from 47 springs daily.

Thousands of years ago, water from rain and snow seeped through cracks in the rocks of Earth's surface. The water was heated by hot, molten rock called magma. This hot water began bubbling back to the surface at an average temperature of 143 degrees Fahrenheit. And it still is, filling pools called thermal springs or hot springs. These pools of water form natural bathing spots.

Over one million gallons of water bubble up each day at Hot Springs, Arkansas.

The Choctaw and the Quapaw used these springs. As early as 1540, European explorers to North America also used these springs. Early leaders of the United States, such as Thomas Jefferson, heard of the springs and urged the government to claim them. In 1832, long before America had any national parks, the government took over the springs and 5,826 acres around them as a federal reservation. Clearly people have always valued these pure, naturally hot waters.

Many people have believed that the Hot Springs and the minerals in the waters have healing powers. They thought that drinking and bathing in the waters would cure sicknesses. While this idea is less popular today, it is true that the waters are pure and free of germs. In fact NASA used the Hot Springs waters to hold the first rocks brought back from the moon to guard them from bacteria.

Today, most people visit Hot Springs National Park because it's fun to bathe in a natural hot tub. About 250,000 people take a refreshing hot spring bath every year.

Hot Springs was the first national health and recreation center in the United States. This photo was taken in 1921, the year the Hot Springs health resort became a national park.

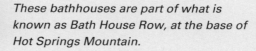

These bathhouses are part of what is known as Bath House Row, at the base of Hot Springs Mountain.

Growing into Tomorrow

The greatest challenges facing Arkansas today are the same ones that were evident in the past. However, Arkansas seems to have come up with some permanent solutions.

Poverty is one of the state's main challenges right now. Only three other states show lower average salary figures than Arkansas. About 16 percent of the population of Arkansas live below the poverty level. Some programs instituted by Bill Clinton toward the end of his tenure as governor have gradually improved these statistics. Clinton's economic programs have helped to attract more high-technology companies to Arkansas. Unemployment is gradually declining while production is gradually increasing. More of these kinds of improvements are needed to have a lasting effect on Arkansas' poverty problems.

Arkansas has been known for its problems with education, but as governor, Clinton also worked to improve that as well. Arkansas now graduates a greater percentage of its high school students than any other

About half of Arkansas is covered with forests. If these forests are carefully protected, Arkansans can hope that their state will always be known as "the Natural State."

The Old Grist Mill in North Little Rock is a reminder that Arkansas can preserve its rustic past while continuing to move into the future.

state in the South. The 1990s brought increases in the state's public school enrollment for the first time in decades. Arkansas' college enrollment rates have also been on the rise, now that the state offers scholarships to lower-income students with academic promise.

Educational reforms have also been creatively combined with reforms in new problem areas such as the environment. One such solution is an organization called WET, which stands for Arkansas Water Education Team. Students involved in WET's program monitor a nearby waterway for pollution and report any changes to the organization. Children in the program gain both the practical skills of using scientific equipment and a genuine respect for the fragile environment around them.

Arkansas has reasons to feel optimistic as it looks to the twenty-first century. The key lies with higher education standards. The bright light of success is made possible only through the power of education.

Circa 8000 B.C. Native Americans called Bluff Dwellers begin to make permanent homes in the Arkansas area.

Circa 1000 B.C. Mound Builders settle in present-day Arkansas.

A.D. 1541 Hernando de Soto explores the Arkansas area.

1673 Father Jacques Marquette and Louis Jolliet come down the Mississippi from Canada, reaching the Arkansas River.

1682 René-Robert Cavelier, Sieur de La Salle, claims the entire Mississippi Valley, including Arkansas, for France.

1686 Henri de Tonti builds a camp at the mouth of the Arkansas River.

1803 The Louisiana Purchase makes present-day Arkansas part of the United States.

1812 The state of Louisiana is formed. The rest of the Louisiana Purchase land becomes the Missouri Territory.

1819 What is now Arkansas and part of Oklahoma becomes the Arkansas Territory.

1820 The Missouri Compromise officially makes Arkansas a slave territory.

1830s Native Americans in the Southeast are forced west on the Trail of Tears.

1832 Arkansas Territory's hot springs are set aside as a public reserve.

1836 Arkansas becomes the 25th state.

1861 The Civil War begins in April. Arkansas withdraws from the Union in May.

1863 Union forces capture Little Rock. Arkansas Confederates move the new state government to Washington, Arkansas.

1868 Arkansas is readmitted to the Union.

1874 The present state constitution is adopted. Joseph Brooks forces Governor Elisha Baxter out of the Arkansas State House at gunpoint. Democrats win the state government back from the Radical Republicans.

1917 Almost seventy thousand Arkansas soldiers serve in World War I.

1921 Oil is discovered near El Dorado. Hot Springs National Park is established.

1927 The Mississippi and Arkansas rivers flood severely, ruining farms in the area.

1930 A severe drought ruins crops across the state. The Great Depression hits the nation.

1931 Hattie Caraway becomes the first woman to be elected to the United States Senate.

1941 The "King Biscuit Time" blues show is started on KFFA in Helena.

1957 Federal troops are sent to enforce integration of Little Rock Central High School.

1967 Winthrop Rockefeller takes office as the first Republican governor of Arkansas since Reconstruction.

1971 The McClellan-Kerr Arkansas River Navigation System opens the river from Mississippi to Oklahoma.

1979 Bill Clinton takes office as governor of Arkansas.

1983 Bill Clinton is reelected as governor.

1986 Helena hosts its first annual King Biscuit Blues Festival.

1992 Governor Bill Clinton is elected President of the United States.

The diamond shape of the state flag represents Arkansas as the only diamond-producing state. The three stars below the state name stand for the three countries—France, Spain, and the United States—that have owned the land of Arkansas. The star above the state name represents the Confederacy. Twenty-five white stars border the diamond in a blue band, representing Arkansas as the twenty-fifth state.

Arkansas Almanac

Nickname. The Natural State

Capital. Little Rock

State Bird. Mockingbird

State Flower. Apple blossom

State Tree. Pine tree

State Motto. *Regnat Populus* (The People Rule)

State Anthem. "Arkansas"

State Abbreviations. Ark. (traditional); AR (postal)

Statehood. June 15, 1836, the 25th state

Government. Congress: U.S. senators, 2; U.S. representatives, 4. State Legislature: senators, 35; representatives, 100. Counties: 75

Area. 53,104 sq mi (137,528 sq km), 27th in size among the states

Greatest Distances. north/south, 240 mi (386 km); east/west, 276 mi (444 km)

Elevation. Highest: Magazine Mountain, 2,753 ft (839 m). Lowest: 55 ft (17 m), along the Ouachita River

Population. 1990 Census: 2,362,239 (3% increase over 1980), 33rd among the states. Density: 44 persons per sq mi (17 persons per sq km). Distribution: 53% urban, 47% rural. 1980 Census: 2,286,418

Economy. *Agriculture:* broilers (young chickens), eggs, beef and dairy cattle, soybeans, rice, cotton, hay, corn, wheat, sorghum grain. *Manufacturing:* food products, electrical equipment and machinery, paper products. *Mining:* natural gas, oil, bromine

State Seal

State Flower: Apple blossom

State Bird: Mockingbird

Annual Events

★ Winter Wings Weekend at Lake Chicot State Park (February)

★ American Fiddlers Jamboree in Harrison (March)

★ Arkansas Folk Festival in Mountain View (April)

★ Diamond Festival in Murfreesboro (May)

★ Summer Solstice at Toltec Mounds State Park (June)

★ Rodeo of the Ozarks in Springdale (July)

★ International Children's Festival at Wildwood Park for the Performing Arts (September)

★ Arkansas State Fair and Livestock Show in Little Rock (October)

★ King Biscuit Blues Festival in Helena (October)

★ Storytelling and Folk Music Festival in Springdale (November)

★ Ozark Christmas in Mountain View (December)

Places to Visit

★ Arkansas Railroad Museum in Pine Bluff

★ Blanchard Springs Caverns, near Mountain View

★ Blues Corner in Helena

★ Children's Museum of Arkansas in Little Rock

★ Crater of Diamonds State Park in Murfreesboro

★ Fort Smith National Historic Site

★ Hot Springs National Park

★ Mid-America Museum in Hot Springs

★ Old State House in Little Rock

★ Ozark Folk Center in Mountain View

★ Parkin Archaeological State Park in Parkin

★ Plantation Agriculture Museum in Scott

3 0060 0002331 4

African Americans, 13, 14, 34–35, 36
  discrimination against, 15–16, 17–18, 20–23
agriculture, 11, 16, 17, 25, 26–27
Anderson, Sam, 37
Arkansas Folk Festival, 33
Arkansas National Guard, 18, 20
Arkansas Post, 10
Arkansas River, 10, 16, 18, 45
Arkansas Territory, 11, 12
Arkansas Water Education Team (WET), 44
Baxter, Elisha, 15
blues, 36–39
Bluff Dwellers, 9
Brooks, Joseph, 15, 45
Brown, Dee Alexander, 35
Caraway, Hattie, 16, 45
Cash, Johnny, 34
Choctaw, 41
Civil War, 13, 14, 45
Cleaver, Eldridge, 34
Clinton, Bill, 19, 43, 45
Clinton, Hillary, 19
Confederacy, 12–13, 14–15
Conway, James S., 12
cotton, 11, 25, 26–27
Cotton, James, 37
Country Music Hall of Fame, 34
Crater of Diamonds State Park, 35
Democrats, 15
de Soto, Hernando, 9–10, 45
Dillard's, 28
Eckford, Elizabeth, 20, 21, 22
education, 14, 17–18, 19, 20–23, 43–44
Eisenhower, Dwight D., 18, 21
environment, 43, 44
Faubus, Orval E., 17, 18, 20, 22
Fiddlers Jamboree, 33
Fletcher, John Gould, 34
folk art, 33

France, 10, 11
gold, 10
Great Britain, 10, 11
Great Depression, 16–17, 30, 45
Green, Ernest, 22
Helena, 33, 36, 37, 38, 39, 45, 47
Hot Springs Mountain, 41
Hot Springs National Park, 40–41, 45
  Bath House Row, 41
Indian Territory, 12
industry, 17
James, Elmore, 37
J. B. Hunt Transport, 30–31
Jefferson, Thomas, 41
Jim Crow laws, 15
Johnson, Robert, 37
Jolliet, Louis, 10, 45
King, B. B., 37
King Biscuit Blues Festival, 33, 36–39, 45
Ku Klux Klan, 15
Lake Ouachita, 35
La Salle, Sieur de, 10, 45
Lincoln, Abraham, 12, 13, 14
Little Rock, 12, 13, 19, 20, 21, 33
  Quapaw Quarter, 11
Little Rock Central High School, 17–18, 20–23, 45
Little Rock Convention Center, 25
Little Rock Nine, 17–18, 20–23
Livin' on the Levee, 33
Lockwood, Robert Jr., 37
Louis XIV, King, 10
Louisiana, 10, 11, 45
lumber industry, 6, 26
manufacturing, 11, 16, 17, 19, 25–26
Marquette, Jacques, 10, 45
McClellan-Kerr Arkansas River Navigation System, 18, 45
McNeil, Marie, 22–23
mining, 16, 17, 27
Mississippi Delta, 36

Mississippi River, 10, 16, 18, 36, 45
Missouri Compromise, 11–12, 45
Mound Builders, 9
Musselwhite, Charlie, 39
Native Americans, 9, 10, 12, 35, 41
Old Grist Mill, 44
Ouachita Mountains, 40
Ozark Mountains, 6, 9, 33, 35
Perkins, Pinetop, 37
petroleum industry, 6, 27
plantations, 11
population, 11, 12
Porterfest, 34
Quapaw, 10, 41
Radical Republicans, 14–15
Randolph, Vance, 35
Reconstruction, 14, 15, 16
Republicans, 15, 18
Revolutionary War, 10
Rockefeller, Winthrop, 18
Roosevelt, Franklin D., 17
Seals, Son, 38
segregation, 17–18, 20–23
service industries, 27–29
settlers, 10, 11, 12
sharecroppers, 14
slavery, 11–13
Slim, Sunnyland, 37
Spain, 9–10
statehood, 12
Still, William Grant, 34–35
Tonti, Henri de, 10, 45
tourism, 29
transportation, 12
Wal-Mart, 28
Walton, Sam, 28–29
Washington, Arkansas 13, 45
Whitney, Eli, 11
Williamson, Sonny Boy, 36, 37, 38
  Sonny Boy Blues Society, 39
World War I, 16
World War II, 17